COFFEE DAYS
WHISKEY NIGHTS

CYRUS PARKER

Hero, 51 Gower Street, London, WC1E 6HJ
hero@hero-press.com | www.hero-press.com

Internal design © 2018 Central Avenue Marketing Ltd.
Cover illustration by Michelle Halket

Originally published in 2018 by Central Avenue Publishing, an imprint of
Central Avenue Marketing Ltd.
www.centralavenuepublishing.com
Print ISBN 978-1-80031-9-684
Ebook ISBN 978-1-80031-9-677

for those struggling to simply be.

coffee days whiskey nights contains sensitive material relating to the following topics:

anxiety and depression, alcohol use, death, disordered eating, gender dysphoria, toxic relationships and potentially more.

please remember to practice self-care before, during, and after reading

when i rise in the morning
and feel the sunlight kiss my skin,
it tells me,

"today is going to be a good day.
you are going to be okay.
you are loved.

i promise."

when i lie awake late into the night
and feel the moonlight wash over me,
it asks me,

"was today a good day?
do you feel okay?
tell me what is weighing so heavily

on your soul."

on the good days, i make

coffee as soon as i wake,

and like i do my creamer,

i pour my hopes and dreams

into poetry with a heavy hand.

on the bad nights, i fill

a glass with whiskey

and let my fears and nightmares

singe my fingertips the same way

the first sip ignites my every nerve.

living can be a burdensome thing that even
the strongest people may struggle to carry.

it is when i find myself crumbling underneath
the weight of it all and am ready to call it quits

that i remind myself that real strength lies
in having courage to ask for a helping hand.

you can tell so much about a person by the way they talk. how they tell a story, the words they use, the words they choose not to use.

i like to think i'm as good at reading people as a writer is at reading their own characters, but i don't always get it right.

i've let some into my life, my home, whose words taste of cotton candy in the daylight, but drip like venom under cover of night.

i'm learning to forgive myself in these situations, but more importantly, i'm learning the difference between those who deserve to be let inside, and those who are lucky enough that i answered the door.

i refuse to be handed things.

i will earn my seat at the table

rather than entertain a courtesy

invite. i know my worth,

and everything i have to offer.

i belong here.

i have uttered this mantra

so many times that my tongue

has memorized the shape of each letter,

but the words carry as much meaning

as a book filled entirely with blank pages.

no prayer, no poem, no hymn—

no matter how many times

it's written, recited, repeated—

can turn fiction into reality.

you won't fit into some places, and that's okay. if we all fit into the same places, then we'd all be the same person. the beauty of humanity is that, no matter how alike we might be, you are still the only you in existence.

i am an all-or-nothing type of person, which is to say
i never love anyone or anything halfway—and i can't
tell if that is halfway good or halfway bad.

why settle for merely a head in the clouds
when your potential is as infinite as the universe?

no matter how much we think
we're in control, life is
there to humble us. carefully
constructed plans come tumbling
down like a preschooler's blocks.
sparks become wildfires.
raindrops become floodwater.
snowflakes become avalanches.
tropical storms become hurricanes.
egos become bombs.
no matter how well you've prepared,
you're left with the task of sifting
through the wreckage, salvaging
what you can, and rebuilding
everything you've known,
piece by piece, block by block.

the heart is as much a mirror as a window, but if you aren't willing to accept what is right before your eyes, it is just as easily a wall.

i'm becoming good friends with four o'clock in the morning. four o'clock is the best listener someone could ask for. three o'clock is fine, but there's something hungry, needy, about four. this desperate longing to hear everything there is to be said before the hour is up, because five o'clock is for the living—it's for getting clothed in the dark and sipping hastily brewed coffee out of travel mugs. it's for quiet drives on empty roads and sitting in parking lots convincing yourself you're going to make it through the next eight hours. it's for realizing that in order to live,

you must first survive

five o'clock is for the living and today i will live
because if i don't do it, nobody else will do it for me.
today i will be conscious of every breath that passes in
and out of these lungs, because these breaths belong to
me and me alone. i'm tired of drifting aimlessly in the
wind, waiting to be carried from one place to another.
who's to stop me from becoming the wind myself?
who's to stop me from shaking some leaves loose?
who's to stop me from making waves? my breath is of
the very same wind that ruffles a bird's feathers and
makes wishes whispered into dandelion seeds take
flight.

i am not afraid to fly.

my entire existence is a contradiction of itself.
i hate leaving the house, but i love to travel.

i spend my day counting calories to counteract my
need to consume until there's nothing left.

i was born into skin that i want nothing more
than to tear off and reshape into something new.

i crave companionship but never feel compelled
to reach out to those i care about.

i am a hopeless romantic, but i have an inability to
express love in a way that makes people feel loved.

i make jokes about dying,
when all i want to do is feel alive.

just because something is broken doesn't mean it can't be fixed. realizing there's a problem is half the battle, but knowing when to hold yourself accountable is the most important part of the equation.

I know I haven't lived up to your expectations, but you haven't lived up to mine, either. the difference is, only one of us is willing to admit our shortcomings.

how many of us stop to consider the fact that the
sun isn't the largest star, but simply the closest? it's a
meaningless fact tucked away in the back of our minds
that most of us never really give any weight to, and
i think that's why it's so easy for us to put people on
pedestals, to conflate the importance of an individual
with the proximity of their touch.

i think about

all the parts of me i changed

for others

and wonder who

it is i'd be

if i had just stayed true

to myself.

they say a picture is worth a thousand words,
but sometimes the clearest pictures are painted
by the words that go unspoken.

it's far too easy to make excuses for the person

that hurts you, and that is why you feel trapped.

sometimes, protecting yourself means doing

the hard thing, and sometimes, the hard thing

is cutting yourself off from them in every way.

i spend an awful lot of time thinking about writing
and not actually doing it. it's not that i don't want to—
sometimes, i just can't find the strength. the strength
to stand up, to walk to wherever i've last stuffed my
laptop, to pick it up, to carry it to my desk, to lift open
the screen and power it on, to open the word document
i've been burying my feelings in. sometimes i feel like
i don't write enough to call myself a writer. sometimes
i don't think i'm poetic enough to call myself a poet.
sometimes i don't think i feel enough to call myself
human, but i'm here—breathing—so that must count
for something.

you ask me for more time

like your fingers aren't wrapped

around my throat, crushing

my windpipe, keeping me

from the air i need to live.

i can only give you so much

time before there isn't any left.

what happens when
no matter how loud you scream,
you're the only one who hears it?

what happens when
you try to make waves
but they're swallowed up by a tsunami?

what happens when
you think you've hit rock bottom
but the bottom keeps falling out?

i'm trying to stay hopeful,
but every day is a little bit
darker than the last, and if i can't

climb my way out of this hole,
i may drag everything
else down with me.

my inner circle has gotten so small

that i can count everyone in it on one

hand, and i'm okay with that.

there are worse things than watching

the people who fail to see your worth

seeing themselves out of it.

i am a hostage

       and anxiety

is my captor,   except

there is no ransom

     that can free me,

        no negotiating

with the villain of this story,

     because it doesn't operate

        with any sort of logic.

    it   silently   seizes

my voice/my thoughts/my life,

bending me until

i'm about to   break,

      and then releases me

when it gets bored

     but never for very long,

because it's always nearby—

    on the phone

      in the passenger seat

        in the car door slamming outside

      in the creaks and groans of the house,

   an uninvited guest

who always stays a little too long.

I bottle my emotions inside empty whiskey bottles that stand atop kitchen cabinets. don't be fooled by the fairy lights glowing in them, though—there's nothing enchanting to be found there.

i feel like i'm spiraling.

at least i'm feeling *something*.

regret tastes like that bottle of six-month-old
blood-orange vodka that sits on top of the refrigerator,
behind the bunch of brown bananas. but the whiskey
is gone and there is no other escape. the acidic burn
sets my tongue on fire. the tangy aftertaste that has me
wishing—praying—that bile will wash it away. i don't
know how i got like this—this vacuum swallowing
anything and everything within its reach in hopes of
filling this emptiness. if i'm not trying to pour alcohol
inside of it, i'm trying to stuff it full of food. i always
seem to want more than i need of everything, but
nothing is enough. nothing is ever enough.

there is so much life to be lived, but we must find the will to live it.

oh, what a mess you've become.
if only you didn't dream so much.

isn't it sad when falling out with a friend isn't a heartbreaking tragedy, but something as regular and mundane as coffee in the morning?

it's so damn hard to grapple with how quickly the tide changes. one moment, i'm wrapped up to my chest in its embrace, and the next, i'm left cold, wet, and alone.

i sometimes wonder about the monotony
of life—the metronome-like regularity

of routine,
of responsibility.

what is the meaning of all this living
when there will come a time

where not a single soul
will remember who i am?

are we all meant to be
such impermanent things?

these ink-stained hands may never give me
the freedom i so desperately long for.

having everything does not stop the want, the need, the hunger, while we are in the process of imploding into ourselves. a black hole doesn't care how many stars it's devoured. all it knows is the need to consume.

isn't that human nature, though?
to find comfort

in the things that destroy us,
to mask the pain

with something even more
hideous,

so we might feel a little less
ugly

when we look at ourselves
in the mirror,

when they look at us
from the outside in.

hiding behind a face
that isn't our own

may make it easier
to get through the day —

what lies beneath will make
the night that much harder.

if you will not weather the storm with me,

perhaps it is time to let it wash this away.

erasing someone from a life is like erasing pencil from paper—no matter how hard we scrub each line away, there will always be a faint trace, an afterimage, of what was once there.

one day, i will not have to hide my pride in the back of a closet in fear of others' eyes.

no matter the size of my clothes,

no matter how well they fit,

my body is the most

uncomfortable thing i wear.

i try to make myself as small as possible, to leave a footprint that is faint, to become invisible without actually disappearing. this body has never really felt like it belonged, so i won't let it take up any more space than it already does.

i live in a house made of mirrors at the intersection of gender dysphoria and binge eating disorder.

i am careful not to throw stones at those in other fragile homes, but it becomes increasingly difficult to hold back my arm when they tell me how i should feel about myself.

it's hard to be positive about this body when each pound makes me that much more aware of every ounce of masculinity my bones carry.

i want the freedom of being able to walk the new york city streets without feeling compelled to throw myself through a window every time i catch my reflection in one.

when people walking those same streets pass me by, i want them to see, not a gender, but a person, who just like them, is simply trying to find a degree of comfort in their own skin.

how much better it must feel to be nothing at all
than to be everything i can't stand.

i don't dream anymore.
i'm not even haunted
by nightmares, these days.

when i was a child, i was
terrorized nightly by images of
shattered windows and gloved hands,

of drifting aimlessly down the flooded
road of a ghost town
without a single soul in sight.

those days are long gone now,
and it's because
i now know that reality

is far more frightening
than anything my mind
could conjure.

notes
7/23/19
6:09 a.m.:

the sun burns
when you've convinced yourself
you're not worthy of its light.

i'm drunk and the lights are out.
is this divine intervention?
a sign from above to stop
me from going too far?

i'm not so egotistical as to believe
there is a divine entity who cares
enough to play the role of overprotective
bartender in my little sob story.

i walk out into the black night and lie
down underneath the big dipper.

i think about both everything and nothing,
and wonder if i deserve any of this—
the stars in the sky, the beauty
of the universe, the air in my lungs.

i decide that if i don't now,

i will one day.

i opened a fortune cookie one afternoon and it said something to the effect of "do what you love to do," and i had to stop and think for a moment because i'm not sure exactly what that is anymore. once upon a time, every single pore on my body oozed passion, but now, i can't squeeze out even a drop.

that feeling you get when you open a new book for the first time, or watch a favorite movie, or play a favorite video game. the feeling you get when you accidentally wake up just in time to catch the sunrise and remember that every day is a new adventure to be excited about.

i want to feel that again. no, i *will* feel that again.

death has been on my mind
a lot more than usual, lately.
not dying, but being dead.
not because i want to die,
but because i know i will.

and as with everything i do, i want
to be prepared for the day my time
comes. i want to make sure that my
loved ones know they are loved.

i want to know that i've done
everything that i've set out
to do in my life. i want to know
that i've made a difference
to someone. anyone. you?

i want to know without a shadow
of a doubt that i've left my mark
on this world, even when there isn't
a single soul left to see it.

the equinoxes show us that we can't have light without the dark, but the solstices show us that they don't always exist in equal parts. sometimes, there is more darkness than light. let us remember that the light will one day outlast the dark.

we are not simply the culmination of our actions,
but the sum of the lives we've touched by living ours.

there are things i expected from you that you couldn't give me, so now i give them to myself.

be guarded, but not so much

that you lock yourself away

in a cage of your own creation.

there is this flawed concept that so many of us
subscribe to:

old-you/new-you

old-you laid the groundwork for the person you are
today.

old-you learned and grew and evolved to get you to
this point.

without old-you, there is no new-you.

don't strive for a different version of yourself.
strive for a better version of yourself.

the person you are right now
is not the person you were

10 years ago
10 months ago
10 weeks ago
10 days ago
10 seconds ago.

you are a work in progress.
learning and growing,
healing and evolving

every second
of every minute
of every day.

wake up early.

watch the sunrise.

go for a walk.

visit a new café.

drink lots of coffee.

take the scenic route to work.

walk aimlessly around a bookstore.

read something.

write something.

find your passion.

dive into it headfirst.

dare to dream

big.

bigger.

inhale.

exhale.

own the day.

every time i look to the moon for guidance, it reminds
me that there is so much more to life than the here and
now — that we are so much more than a single moment
in time.

cultivate a space that is yours and yours alone.
fill it with all your favorite things.

a place that
—when the world becomes too much to bear—

will be waiting for you with open arms
whenever you need a place to call home.

every single day is a war to wear this skin a little more comfortably than the last, and while i'm certain this body will never resemble a home, i refuse to feel like a stranger in it anymore.

the new year is quickly approaching, and this will be the year i break the cycle of making resolutions and failing to keep them.

just like the promise of a new day doesn't fix yesterday's problems, a new year doesn't fix the problems of the one before.

a new year, like a new day, is simply an opportunity to write the greatest chapter in your story, but you can't write that chapter unless you first pick up the pen.

do not let your fear
of burning up
in the atmosphere
stop you from

chasing

the

stars.

today we clean out the fridge.

i get a chance to dispose of all the rot taking up space:
the moldy oranges,

the soggy salads left from the last time i said,
"i'm going on a diet,"

the coffee creamer i let go to waste because i got sick of
the flavor.

there's a shelf in the door where half a bottle of jack sits
alongside the ingredients to make manhattans.

"do you want to keep any of it?" she asks.

it doesn't take me long to make up my mind. i grab
the bottle of whiskey, pour it down the drain, chase it
with the bottle of vermouth, before finishing things off
by disposing of the bitters and maraschino cherries.
nothing is more cathartic than making the decision to
take back your life.

tear open the night sky,

bottle up all the starlight

your fingertips can reach,

and tuck it away deep beneath

your rib cage, where no one

can ever take it away.

some say my generation
is too wrapped up in social media
to live their lives, but that's not
what i see. i see a generation
who desperately wants to cling
to every precious moment
because we know the good ones
are so few and far between.
i see a generation who knows
that life is a fleeting thing, and
there's only so much time to leave
behind something that says, *"i was here.*
i existed." but more importantly,
"i lived."

snap one too many selfies.
send those tweets saved in your drafts.
post that photo of your pumpkin spice latte.
do all of the things that make you happy
and share each one of them with the world,
because we could all use
a little more joy in our lives.

take back your favorite songs. reclaim your favorite
places. scrub their fingerprints from everything they've
ever touched, and heal. heal. heal.

you don't owe everyone every part of you.
even the most honest hearts hold secrets inside.

say yes to more things outside
of your comfort zone.

say no to more things that do not
bring inner peace.

every relationship is a learning experience, but this one
will be more than just another lesson.

i am picking up all the pieces you took for granted, and
i am giving them to someone who appreciates every
jagged edge.

i will survive despite you.

i will thrive to spite you.

i make my morning coffee the long way, the slow way,
to force myself to simply *be*.

grind the beans.
boil the water in a gooseneck kettle.
pour just enough to saturate the grounds.
give them time to bloom.

it is called the bloom because the grounds swell up and
out like a blossom in spring.

a poet must've named this step in a moment of
inspiration,

because if flowers can bloom, and coffee can bloom,
then people can bloom, too, if only given the chance to
stop and simply *be*.

you existed before them.

you will exist after them.

our mornings begin with you telling me to make
you coffee, and me jokingly replying, *"please?"* and
sunlight pours into our living room as we sip from
our mugs and watch our cats chase each other around
the house. sometimes we talk. sometimes we just
enjoy the coffee and each other's presence. and there
is this sense of serenity that fills the air in these quiet
moments that i wouldn't trade for the whole world,
because what is the world against everything the
universe encompasses? and you, gorgeous, put even
the universe to shame.

you help make all these coffee days
and whiskey nights worth living.

the greatest gift you can give yourself

is permission to be. as you are. without conditions.

this is me,

                      forging my own path.

this is me,

                      building my own future.

this is me,

                      finding my own success.

this is me,

                      writing my own ending.

As always, some thank-yous are in order:

Thank you to Michelle Halket, Central Avenue Publishing, and IPG for taking a chance on me and giving me the opportunity to put *coffee days whiskey nights* out into the world.

Thank you to Aaron Kent, who both inspired and first published a version of the poem on page 75. You can find the original in the *Poetic Interviews* anthology, available through Broken Sleep Books.

To my gorrrrrrgeous wife, amanda lovelace, thank you. Thank you for existing. Thank you for the infinite amounts of love and support you've given me. Thank you for the invaluable advice and guidance. Most importantly, thank you for being you.

And last—but certainly not least—thank you, the reader, as well as everyone who has ever supported me and my work in any way. Without all of you, I wouldn't be fortunate enough to keep doing this.

Cyrus Parker is a non-binary poet and storyteller, as well as the author of multiple collections of poetry, including *DROPKICKromance* and *masquerade*. Hailing from a small coastal town in New Jersey alongside wife and poetess amanda lovelace—and their cats—Cyrus can usually be found at local coffee shops not writing when they should be, or at home sipping the occasional glass of whiskey while lamenting over the cancellation of *Marvel's Jessica Jones*.

cyrusparker.com

@cyrusparker

cyrus parker

in conversation with

amanda lovelace

al: Tell me about the inspiration behind your newest poetry
collection, *coffee days whiskey nights*.

cp: I think the initial idea for *coffee days whiskey nights* came
from a couple of photos I took from our hotel room in New
York City a few years back. In the first, I photographed my
morning cup of coffee on the windowsill with the city as its
backdrop. The second photo was staged the exact same way,
but instead of a coffee cup, there was a whiskey bottle, and
the city was lit up at nighttime. I think I posted the photos
online together with the caption "coffee mornings, whiskey
nights" and immediately thought how cool a title that could
be for a collection of poems. I know it's currently 2020, but
I still have a file on my laptop named "coffee mornings,
whiskey nights" that dates back to 2017, which means
I've been sitting on this idea since before my first poetry
collection even hit shelves!

al: How is *coffee days whiskey nights* different from your other
two poetry collections, *DROPKICKromance* (2018, Andrews
McMeel) and *masquerade* (2019, Andrews McMeel)?

cp: I think the biggest difference between my previous
works and *coffee days whiskey nights* is that this one isn't
based directly on my life. I consider *DROPKICKromance* and

masquerade to be almost poetic memoirs, whereas *coffee days whiskey nights* doesn't share that same narrative structure. The poems in *coffee days whiskey nights* are just as personal and absolutely inspired by my own feelings and lived experiences, but I wouldn't consider this one memoir-esque the way I do my previous works. And as with all of my poetry collections, I've tried to do something stylistically different. *DROPKICKromance* played around with page alignment and utilized tagline titles, while *masquerade* had more traditional titles on the top and included some of my own artwork. *coffee days whiskey nights*, on the other hand, has no titles at all, and we've included alternating black and white pages to illustrate the day/night concept I went with in this book.

al: I'm fascinated by the format of this new collection! The alternating black and white pages really add to the ambience of the overall reading experience, in my opinion. Was this design choice always your intention, and do you think it works in the way you intended?

cp: Thank you! The alternating black and white pages were not always part of the plan, actually. Initially, I imagined a book that looked somewhat like my journal, so there would've been some poems done in my own messy handwriting, as well as some sketches (think *masquerade*) to really give it that journal feel. However, the idea of playing off the title and splitting the poems into day and night really resonated with me, and I thought it would be super cool if the day poems were black text on white paper and the night poems would be white text on black paper. When I pitched the book to Michelle at Central Avenue, I proposed both ideas as separate concepts, and we decided to move forward with the day/night concept, which I think worked out even better than I had envisioned!

al: How do you take your coffee?

cp: With oat milk and Sweet'N Low!

al: How many cups of coffee do you drink in a day? Is there a set number and a routine, or does it vary?

cp: I'd say somewhere between three and five cups a day. I do have a bit of a routine in the morning where I make myself a piccolo latte as soon as I wake up, to get that jolt of caffeine in before I do my daily DDPY workouts, and I always have a cup of coffee after I finish. Two o'clock is lunch-and-latte hour in our house, as you know, and I usually manage to get another cup or two in before the day is up, but it's never less than three for me.

al: What's your favorite brand of whiskey?

cp: Right now, I'm in love with Asbury Park Distilling Co.'s Double Barrel Bourbon. Support local distilleries!

al: I have to know: which poet—either dead or alive—would you want to have a chat with over a glass of bourbon?

cp: I have to go with Edgar Allan Poe. I'd love to spend some time picking his brain and learning of all the horrors that live inside. Emily Dickinson is a very close second!

al: What is the writing process like for your poetry collections? Can you walk us through from start to finish?

cp: I almost always start with a title, and with the title comes the theme and concept. From there, I start flipping through my journals and scrolling through my files, and begin compiling existing poems that go well with the theme of the collection. Once I have the bones of the book in place, I write more poems and start filling in the missing pieces until I feel I have a cohesive book. Then comes beta reading and editing and all the really fun stuff.

al: Do you have any new collections—or maybe even novels—in the works? Can we expect anything else from you soon? *fingers crossed*

cp: I'm always writing poems, so another poetry collection from me is inevitable—it's just a matter of when! As for novels, I've been toying with a fantasy novel since 2014 and I really want to get the ball rolling on it. I've been doing a lot of brainstorming lately and have begun the process of plotting it out, so I'm hoping to make it happen sooner, rather than later.

al: And finally, which five items would someone need to place in a pentagram in order to summon you? (I'm sure I can refer to the title of your new collection for two of them!)

cp: Coffee, whiskey, my cats, my signature beanie, and you!